PARENT CONTRACTS
TO IMPROVE SCHOOL BEHAVIOR

BY SUSAN E. SMITH

SUSAN E. SMITH

SUSAN E. SMITH has a B.S. in Elementary Education, and an M. Ed. in Counseling from the University of Oklahoma, and an Ed. M. in Developmental Disabilities from Rutgers University. She is a counselor with the Ft. Lee Public Schools in New Jersey.

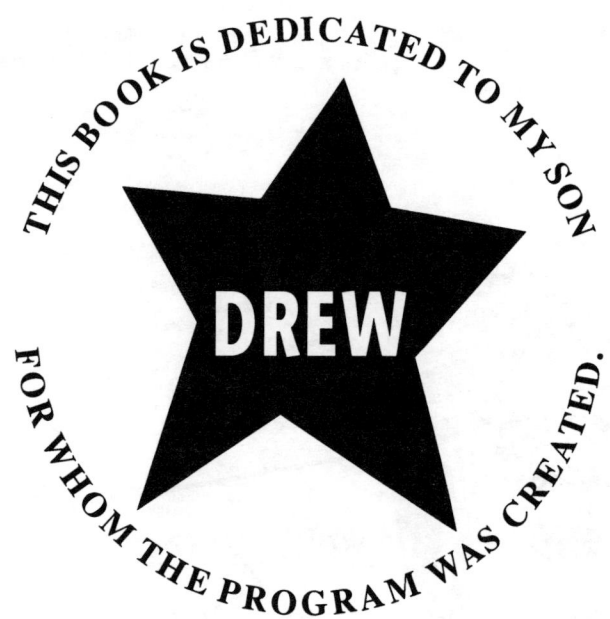

THIS BOOK IS DEDICATED TO MY SON DREW FOR WHOM THE PROGRAM WAS CREATED.

copyright © 1997
mar•co products, inc.

Published by
mar•co products, inc.
1443 Old York Road
Warminster, PA 18974
1-800-448-2197

Library of Congress Catalog Card Number: 96-079862

ISBN: 1-57543-021-5

Printed in the U.S.A.

CONTENTS

HOW TO USE THE PARENT CONTRACTS TO IMPROVE SCHOOL BEHAVIOR PROGRAM

One of the major concerns that teachers and counselors have is getting parents to work with them on behavior changes that are needed at school. One of the major concerns that parents have is knowing how to help their child make behavior changes at school. *Parent Contracts To Improve School Behavior* can be the answer.

Most parenting books mention behavior contracts, in one way or another, but most parents have little knowledge of what constitutes a behavior contract program, or how to go about starting such a program. That is the purpose of this program. Parent-child contracts can be extremely effective when they are used to improve school behaviors, family responsibilities, chores, and the child's general behavior.

This program contains detailed information (pages 7-8, 11-14, 17-18, and 23-26) about contracts for teachers and counselors that can be reproduced for parents. Included in the information are examples of school-related target behaviors (pages 15-16) and grade level suggestions for recognizing the child's achievement (pages 27-28). There are also ready-to-use reproducible contracts (pages 9-10), charts (19-22), and awards (pages 29-32).

WHEN TO USE A PARENT CONTRACT

Parent contracts will be useful when *both* the teacher and the parent agree that a school-related behavior is affecting the child's social or academic progress. Seriousness is essential. Both the teacher and the parent *must* believe the child has a problem and *both* must be willing to make a serious commitment to facilitate the change.

How To Present The Contract Program To Teachers

The contract program requires teacher cooperation and therefore should be presented to them before giving it to parents. The most efficient way to make teachers aware of the program is to present it at a group meeting. In this way, each teacher hears the same explanation. It should be made clear to the teachers that they may recommend a student for the contract program, or if you see a need for a contract program you will only implement it with their approval. When finished explaining the program, give the teachers a simple pre-prepared form (page 5) which will let them participate or not participate in the program.

If it isn't possible to present the program at a group meeting, then discuss the program individually with teachers who have students that you feel could profit from this type of program.

PARENT CONTRACT PROGRAM

I understand:

✔ **That I must agree to a contract program for a student before the parent is approached.**

✔ **That I may refer students for the contract program.**

✔ **My responsibilities if the program is initiated.**

☐ I wish to participate in the *Parent Contract Program.*

☐ I do not wish to participate in the *Parent Contract Program.*

Please return this form to _____ by _____ .

How To Present The Contract Program To A Parent

In most cases, the contract will be presented on an individual basis. However, if facilitating a parent group or giving a parent or teacher inservice, the parent contract procedure can be presented to a group. Whether presented individually or in a group, the actual writing of the contract should be done on an individual basis. This ensures the privacy to which the parties involved are entitled.

Read the information presented in the program thoroughly before presenting the format to a parent. If desired, reproduce the information. It can be helpful to give the parent a copy of the procedural information (pages 7-8, 11-14, 17-18, and 23-26) to use while the program is being explained and also to take home for reference after the conference is finished.

Explain to the parent that the teacher is in agreement with the contract program and will work with the parent to help the child correct the misbehavior. If the parent agrees to the contract, write the contract together.

How To Present The Contract Program To The Child

Once the contract is written, the child must be told. This can be done in two ways. One way is to have one person explain the contract to the child. This can be done by either the counselor, teacher, or parent. Another way, which is more effective, is to have a conference which includes the parent, the child, the counselor, and the teacher. When the contract is explained with all parties present, the child is fully aware that everyone involved is working together. This can minimize future misunderstandings.

How To Have Successful Follow-Up

Once the contract is written and the teacher and parent put it into operation, the counselor should follow-up weekly or biweekly with either the teacher or the parent. Since follow-up is essential, it is necessary not to overload the program to the point where follow-up becomes either too cumbersome or impossible.

CONTRACTS

What is a contract?

A contract is a written promise or an agreement. In a contract, two people promise or agree to do very specific things. As adults, we experience contracts as a common activity in our daily lives. When we purchase a home, we contract with a mortgage company or a bank to finance the purchase. The bank or mortgage company promises to loan the money to purchase the home, and we promise to repay the loan on a monthly basis. We enter into contracts to purchase automobiles, use credit cards, obtain employment, and service our appliances. A contract defines a specific goal and clarifies exactly what each person has agreed to do. Responsibilities are clearly stated, as are each person's benefits and possible consequences.

What is a behavior contract?

A behavior contract defines exactly what actions the child and parent are responsible for doing, the benefits or rewards, and in some cases, the consequences for not producing the promised effort. A behavior contract is a commitment between the parent and the child. Behavior contracts for this program are a written agreement between you and your child. The contract will state the exact school-related behavior that your child is expected to improve. The contract also identifies the benefits that you have agreed to provide, when your child improves the school-related behavior as agreed.

What must be done to make a behavior contract work?

The effectiveness of a behavior contract program will depend on how well your child's individual contract and contract program are prepared, how well the behaviors are identified and evaluated, and the intrinsic value of the rewards and positive reinforcements. For these reasons, each part of the contract program must be thoroughly understood.

Is the behavior contract written or oral?

The contract is written and must specify the exact responsibilities of each person who is involved with the agreement. These responsibilities must be put in writing to avoid any misunderstandings. The contract must also be signed by both you and your child. The signatures reinforce that you have made an agreement or a promise to each other.

What is target behavior?

The specific behavior that is to be improved is identified as the goal or target behavior. This target behavior must be very clearly stated, so that your child understands exactly what your expectations are. Not only must the target behavior be very specific, it must also be observable and measurable.

What do I do when my child achieves the target behavior?

You agree to recognize your child in some way. This recognition may be seen as a reward. The recognition which you agree to provide when your child achieves the target behavior must be of value to him/her. It must be stated on the contract, because it is equally as important as the target behavior. Recognizing your child's achievement is basically your "part of the bargain."

What happens when my child does not achieve the target behavior?

In this contract program, there will be no identified consequences for not achieving the target behavior. The consequence will be the withholding of recognition. In some contract programs, there are consequences that are a very important part of the contract. These usually involve some type of privilege that will be lost or denied, if the specific target behavior is not achieved. In this case, if recognition is meaningful to your child, denial of it is usually sufficient.

How long does a contract last?

Your child's contract will be renewed on a weekly basis. Your child's teacher will be responsible for the evaluations of the school-related behavior, which will be recorded on a daily basis. These daily evaluations will be reported to you every Friday. Earned recognition should be given on Friday, or as soon as possible. Each Monday, you should send a new behavior evaluation chart to your child's teacher.

After a period of three or four weeks of successful goal completion, your child's contract will need to be revised. At this point, you may choose to eliminate the contract entirely or decide to make the target behavior increasingly more difficult.

> For example: Johnny has successfully completed all math homework for one month. Johnny's teacher and Johnny's parent agree that they want to change the target behavior to now include completion of both math and English homework.

BEHAVIOR CONTRACT

_____ **agrees to improve**
NAME OF STUDENT

school behavior and promises to _____

_____

_____ .

_____ **agrees to** _____
NAME OF PARENT

_____

when _____ **does as agreed.**

This contract begins on _____ **and ends on** _____ .

SCHOOL BEHAVIOR WILL BE EVALUATED THROUGH WEEKLY EVALUATION REPORTS. SPECIAL RECOGNITION WILL BE GIVEN WEEKLY FOR SUCCESSFUL GOAL COMPLETION.

_____
DATE

_____   _____
PARENT'S SIGNATURE   STUDENT'S SIGNATURE

BEHAVIOR ★ CONTRACT

_____ promises to
NAME OF STUDENT

_____ .

_____**will**_____
NAME OF PARENT

_____

when this promise is kept.

This contract will start on _____

and end on _____ .

_____
DATE

_____   _____
PARENT'S SIGNATURE   STUDENT'S SIGNATURE

TARGET BEHAVIORS

How important is target behavior?

The target behavior is the specific behavior that you want your child to improve. Improvement of the target behavior will be the goal or purpose of the entire contract program. An appropriate and well-defined target behavior is vital to the effectiveness and success of any contract program. Effective goals and target behaviors are specific, well defined, and measurable.

How can I make the target behavior effective and meaningful for my child?

In order to identify an effective and meaningful target behavior, the problem behavior must first be clearly defined. As the parent, you must do two things:

- Identify the problem behavior.
- Decide the exact behavior change that you expect from your child.

    For example: Suppose that your child received all D's on a report card, and you know he/she is capable of much higher academic achievement.

- What is the problem? (The problem can be identified, in general terms, as poor grades in school.)

- What is the actual problem? (More specifically, the actual problem is all D's on a report card.)

- What is the goal you want your child to reach? (In general terms, a goal might be stated that your child should improve report card grades.)

- What do you as a parent expect? (You, as a parent, however, really do expect all B's. This would be a reasonable parent expectation, if your child is perfectly capable of earning all B's.)

- What is the goal? (The goal should very clearly state your perfectly reasonable expectation which is all B's on the report card.)

The target behavior which clearly states that you expect all B's is much better defined and more easily measured than the goal which simply stated that your child should improve report card grades. As a parent, you have stated reasonable expectations. Your child now knows exactly what behavior is expected. There is no confusion and there are no misunderstandings. Your expectations are reasonable, well defined, and measurable.

What if my child has several different behavior problems?

Many times a child's behavior is generally unacceptable and may include several different behavior problems.

For example: If your child is not doing homework, in general, that problem behavior actually is a combination of the child not completing homework in math, science, English, and social studies.

In this situation, the homework problem may be so large that it must be divided into smaller units, or tasks, in order for systematic behavior improvement to take place.

Always break down large problems into smaller manageable tasks. It is unlikely that your child will be able to improve all of his/her report card grades from D's to B's in only a period of one month or six weeks. It is certainly possible, though, to bring a math grade from a D to a B in a few weeks, and an English grade from a D to a B in a few weeks. By breaking the larger goal into smaller goals, your child can ultimately accomplish the entire larger goal. Obtaining B's in both English and math is a definite improvement from all D's on a report card. It is often necessary to improve behaviors one step at a time. As one step is mastered, a second step is added. Once the child has gotten B's in English and math, the next step would be to work on improving grades in other subjects.

Why is breaking larger tasks into small steps helpful for my child?

Large tasks are often overwhelming, complicated, or confusing to a child. General behaviors are often too difficult for parents to define or quantify. Therefore, many inappropriate or general problem behaviors must be broken down into specific actions or parts that are both measurable and observable. When large tasks are divided into smaller steps, your child will be able to find success with each small and manageable part.

For example: A child may really want to learn to read, but will not be able to accomplish this goal until he/she first learns to identify letters of the alphabet.

If your child finds success and is rewarded as each smaller task is completed, the improved behavior is more likely to be repeated and the larger goal is more likely to be achieved.

What do I need to do in order for my child and me to think alike about a task?

Children often do not evaluate large tasks in the same way as an adult would identify the same task. This can cause problems with goal identification and in evaluations.

For example: A clean room to your child might mean that all toys are put away. To you, however, a clean room is actually a combination of several factors that may include toys put away, a bed that is neatly made, and clothes that are hung up in a closet.

In order for you and your child to think alike about a task, the target behavior must state your exact and reasonable expectations, which are clearly defined for your child's understanding.

For example: The target behavior for a clean room must specify that toys are put away, clothes are hung up, and the bed is neatly made.

What is the best way for me to communicate with my child?

Whenever possible, state the target behaviors in the positive, rather than in the negative. If you are looking for a positive behavior change and you expect a positive behavior change, then state the target behavior in the way that you expect your child to perform.

> For example: Instead of saying, "John will not miss any homework assignments," say, "John will complete all English assignments for one week."

You want positive behavior and improvement, so let your child know exactly what positive behavior that you expect to see. You expect more than just an improvement in spelling grades, you expect an 80% or better on all spelling tests. Your child will respond much better when he/she understands exactly what is expected of him/her.

How can I measure my child's progress?

Goals and target behaviors must be objective and they must be able to be measured.

> For example:

- What is an example of a goal that is not clearly defined? (A goal stating, "Amy will do her homework," is not clearly defined and can be difficult to measure or evaluate.)

- What is an example of a clearly defined goal? (A more specific goal would state that "Amy will do her math homework every night for one week.")

- Why is this statement better than the first one? (In the second statement, the questions "who," "what," and "when," can be answered. In the revised goal statement the "who" is Amy, the "what" is math homework completion, and the "when" is every night for one week.)

- Why is this type of statement easy to measure? (The achievement of the goal can be answered with a simple "yes" or "no." Amy has either completed the math homework every night for one week, or she hasn't.)

- Can goals also include "where" and "how." (Sometimes goals can be so specific that they also include "where" and "how." In this situation, the goal would state that, "Amy will complete her math homework, in her room, every night by 9:00 PM, for one week." Because teachers will be evaluating the child's behaviors at school, "where" and "how" may be difficult to monitor with this program.)

- Always try to create target behaviors that will at least answer "who," "what," and "when."

How can teachers and counselors help me with my child's goals?

When parents find that goal identification is difficult, it is always helpful to meet with their child's teacher and counselor to form a cooperative effort in the development of specific and appropriate goals for school-related behaviors. Teachers and counselors are usually able to provide you with a clearer understanding of your child's behavior in the school setting. They will welcome your support and cooperation, and in many situations behaviors previously identified as general disruptions can be more clearly identified as speaking out of turn, leaving a seat, or interrupting other children who are working.

If the target behaviors and improvement goals that you establish with your child are age appropriate, not too difficult, clearly defined, specific, and measurable, then your child will understand exactly what behavior you expect, and exactly what behavior will receive recognition.

Examples of School-Related Target Behaviors (pages 15-16) will give you some examples of ways to write target behaviors that are clearly defined, specific, and measurable.

Notice that target behaviors or goals are monitored for one week. Once the target behavior is decided upon, the counselor should reproduce one of the *Evaluation Sheets* (pages 19-22) for monitoring your child's behavior. Complete the sheet with your child present. Then the evaluation sheet should be given to the teacher to monitor your child for the week. At the end of the week, the evaluation sheet should be sent home to you.

The counselor can help monitor your child's progress by meeting with him/her on Friday after the evaluation has been received and before it goes home. At that time, additional reinforcement with a written award, a star on a chart, or perhaps a token gift such as a pencil or sticker can give your child another bit of encouragement.

EXAMPLES OF SCHOOL-RELATED TARGET BEHAVIORS

John will complete all math homework, every day, for one week.

Amy will arrive at school by 8:30 AM, every day, for one week.

Andy will not receive a school detention, for one week.

Mary will earn an 80% or higher on all spelling tests, for one week.

José will use appropriate language to all teachers and school staff, for one week.

Tom will have no physical altercations (fights) with other children, at school, for one week.

Billy will not use profanity, during school hours, for one week.

Jane will complete all classroom English assignments, each day, for one week.

Jim will be prepared for science class by bringing all required books, pencils, and papers, for one week.

Juan will speak only when recognized by the teacher, in social studies class, every day, for one week.

Sandra will eat her entire lunch, in the cafeteria, for one week.

Sally will not be verbally abusive (say nasty things) to other children, at school, every day, for one week.

Bobby will walk in the classrooms and halls, every day, for one week.

Mark will remain in the math classroom for the entire class period, every day, for one week.

Stephanie will be in the English classroom by 10:45 AM and 12:45 PM each day, for one week.

Carl will remain in his seat, without talking to other children, from 9:00 AM until 9:45 AM every day, for one week.

Tom will sit in his seat, without kicking the student next to him, every day, for one week.

Timothy will put only things that belong to him in his backpack, every day, for one week.

Joey will hang his coat on the hook every morning, for one week.

Patrick will not tell any tattletales all day, for one week.

Martha will wash her face and hands at 8:45 AM every morning, for one week.

Jonathan will organize his desk at 3:15 PM every day, for one week.

Kate will remember to bring her flute to school on Monday, Wednesday, and Friday, for one week.

Missy's name will not be written on the board for breaking class rules, each day, for one week.

Kevin will sit quietly in the story circle, without touching other children, every day, for one week.

EVALUATIONS

What is the procedure for evaluations?

Each Monday provide your child's teacher with a new evaluation chart. Be sure to have the chart completed with the child's name, dates, and target behavior. Evaluations will be completed each day by your child's teacher or another designated school staff member. Your child will bring the completed and signed behavior evaluation home to you each Friday. Do not complete your part of the contract unless your child's target behavior is accomplished each day.

Several different evaluation charts have been provided for you to use (pages 19-22). You may also enjoy creating your own evaluation charts with your child. Coloring books and activity books are wonderful sources of potential evaluation charts.

Are there any extenuating circumstances which are acceptable?

In the event that the teacher was unable to evaluate the behavior for a specific day, the teacher can indicate N/A and your child is given credit for task completion.

> For example: The target behavior is to complete English homework each night. However, homework was not assigned on a given day.

Other exceptions might include your child's absence from school, a special program or class trip, or a substitute teacher in the classroom.

How exact must the teacher's evaluation be?

Evaluations must always be precise and accurate. Evaluations must meet the exact standards that were established for each target behavior. If your child does not perform the target behavior exactly as it appears on the contract, he/she will not be given credit for completing the task.

The basic rule for evaluations is NO EXCEPTIONS. A contractual agreement does not allow for partial fulfillment or "just this once" exceptions. When exceptions are allowed they:

- violate the meaning of the original agreement.
- confuse the child.
- teach the child to think "sliding by" is acceptable.
- teach the child that standards are flexible.

Is there any way flexibility is acceptable?

Flexibility is acceptable if it has been permitted in your particular contract program. To do this, the contract must clearly state that "Johnny will be on time for school, four out of five days."

What do I do when my child disagrees with the evaluation?

Accurate recording greatly reduces a child's ability to argue for or manipulate for unearned rewards. However, for those times when your child's evaluation chart indicates that the target behavior was not completed, and your child disagrees with you, simply say:

- "I'm sorry that you chose not to do your homework every night. This means that I cannot keep my part of the contract. Let's try our contract again next week as I would very much like to see you succeed. When you succeed, I can keep my part of the contract."

  or

- "When you choose not to complete your homework, I cannot keep my part of the contract because that is the way that our agreement is written."

You are not telling your child something that is not already known. Your child knows he/she did not complete the target behavior and fully understands why you are not keeping your part of the bargain. What your child is doing is trying to wear you down. Do not give in and do not argue with your child.

When should the teacher record evaluations?

Record behavior immediately after it occurs or at a specified evaluation time each day. Consistent and objective recording reduces judgment errors. To make recording easier, the target behavior should be stated so that the evaluation only requires a "yes" for completed or a "no" for not completed.

How do evaluations help my child?

Evaluations will help your child to identify his/her own progress. They will also serve as a reminder to your child that a promise to improve behavior was made, and that his/her efforts to keep this promise are being very closely monitored. Evaluations record your child's level of responsibility for holding up his or her "part of the bargain."

What if the contract does not seem to be working?

Evaluations will measure progress or lack of progress. They will tell you exactly how well your contract program is working. If the evaluations indicate that your child is not having a very high success rate in accomplishing the goal, then perhaps it is necessary to evaluate the contract itself. Decide if:

- Your part of the agreement has significant value for your child.
- The target behavior is too difficult for your child.
- The target behavior is not clearly defined.
- The evaluation method needs to be changed from weekly to daily.

If you need help identifying the problem areas of your contract, consult your child's teacher or counselor.

WEEKLY EVALUATION

Name _____

Week of _____

Target Behavior

_____

_____

_____

	YES	NO
Monday		
Tuesday		
Wednesday		
Thursday		
Friday		

Teacher's Signature_____

Student's Signature_____

STAR CHART

Name _____

Week of _____

Target Behavior _____

_____

_____

Monday	Tuesday	Wednesday	Thursday	Friday

WEEKLY EVALUATION

Name _____

Week of _____

Goal _____

_____

_____

	YES	NO
Monday		
Tuesday		
Wednesday		
Thursday		
Friday		

Teacher's Signature _____

WEEKLY EVALUATION

Name _____

Week of _____

Goal _____

_____

	YES	NO
Monday		
Tuesday		
Wednesday		
Thursday		
Friday		

Teacher's Signature _____

RECOGNITION

Why is recognition important?

Recognizing good behavior is probably the easiest and most important way to bring about positive behavior changes. If positive behaviors are recognized, they are more likely to occur again.

Remember, most of the choices we make in our daily lives are based on positive reinforcement or concern for lack of positive reinforcement. It is unlikely that most people would trudge off to work each day if a paycheck weren't waiting at the end of the week. The recognition given in contract programs will have the same meaning to your child as a paycheck or compliment has to you.

When should recognition be given?

Recognition should be given as soon as possible after the desired behavior occurs.

> For example: If your child has agreed to complete all homework for a period of one week, then the accomplishment of this goal should be recognized as soon as possible after the child has produced evidence that all homework has been completed for one week.

Older children are more capable of delayed gratification, but younger children will often lose interest if not recognized immediately. In fact, very young children may often benefit from a daily award program. Immediate gratification is most effective in producing additional positive behaviors.

Can recognition be given if the target behavior is partially completed?

No. Remember that you have agreed to provide the recognition, only if your child produces the specific behavior. It is important to always be consistent with recognition, so that your child will completely understand exactly what behavior you expect and exactly what recognition will result if the behavior is accomplished. There are NO EXCEPTIONS.

How important is consistency?

Being consistent isn't always easy. Consistency, however, is an absolute necessity for your child's positive behavior change. Your contract must set specific standards, and you and the teacher must stick to these standards each and every time—NO EXCEPTIONS.

Remember, you are a responsible parent who has made a reasonable agreement with your child. Do not lower your reasonable expectations or standards by allowing your child to manipulate you or wear you down. You should not feel guilty for not fulfilling your part of the agreement when your child did not complete the target behavior. Children are happier when their parent's expectations, standards, and limits are very clear and understood.

Which type of recognition is most effective?

The type of recognition which is most effective is one that has a personal meaning or specific value to your child, but is something that may have little or no value to you or another child.

Are rewards and privileges the only way to recognize positive behavior changes?

No. In addition to the promised reward or privilege, there are additional actions that will reinforce the desired behavior change and encourage your child to repeat this changed behavior. Heap on lots of praise, hugs, and kisses. Don't forget to tell your child how much you love and how proud you are of him/her. Make a really sincere big deal about the positive behavior change. Try something like putting a little note in your child's lunch box as a reminder of just how proud you are and how much you are looking forward to another successful week.

Be very specific with your praise, because general praise can sometimes be confusing to a child. Rather than saying, "I am so proud of you," try saying, "I am so proud of you for completing all of your assignments this week." Praise and recognition are natural and logical consequences of good behavior.

What is the difference between praise and encouragement?

There are major differences between praise and encouragement. Praise recognizes the external action such as actually arriving at school on time for each day of the week. It is given when something is done exactly as it was contracted.

Encouragement recognizes the effort that it took for your child to arrive at school on time for each day of the week. Encouragement focuses on your child's efforts, and it is an important way to build the self-confidence that will produce more desired results in the future.

Encouragement can be given when a contract is partially completed. An encouraging parent, when looking at the weekly evaluation sheet, would say, "I see you made it to school on time three times this week," instead of saying, "You didn't get to school on time two days this week."

Speaking in this fashion does not give your child recognition for completing the task, but it also does not "put the child down" for not completing the task. Effective encouragement focuses on your child's efforts and it is an important way to build the self-confidence that will produce more desired results in the future.

Praise is reserved for recognition of a job well done. Encouragement acknowledges the efforts that were required to do the job.

What about negative reinforcement?

Some contract programs include negative reinforcement and punishment.

> For example: If a child does not complete the target behavior a punishment or negative consequence would be to take a child's bicycle away for two days. An example of negative reinforcement would be to take the bicycle away, indefinitely, until the child does produce the desired behavior.

This particular program is designed to use only positive reinforcement. If your child does not complete the target behavior, the withholding of a recognition of value to your child should be adequate.

How will I know which type of recognition will work?

Look at the *Recognition Suggestions* (pages 27-28). These are suggestions made by children of various ages who were asked what they would like to earn, from their parents, for improving test grades. These are suggestions and your child may or may not be interested in them. Your child also might not be interested in a recognition that would have tremendous value to a sibling or a friend. It is permissible to discuss what would be of value to your child. If a recognition does not seem to be of interest, do not hesitate to change it. Recognitions can be changed from one week to the next as long as they are added in writing to the behavior contract. It is also perfectly acceptable to add an additional special recognition or privilege if your child successfully completes the target behavior for an agreed upon number of consecutive weeks. The decision is entirely up to you.

How much money will these recognitions cost?

Some recognitions cost no money at all and those on the suggested list that do, cost $5.00 or less. Do not feel that you must make a financial sacrifice to provide a recognition that will have personal value to your child. Privileges often have more personal value to a child, and yet may have no monetary value at all. Extra TV time, extra telephone privileges, or additional computer game time have no monetary value, but they are privileges that are a delight to most children.

Are there other types of positive reinforcement?

Yes. Awards (pages 29-32) serve as a pleasant reminder that the target behavior was completed and are another important form of positive reinforcement. Hang the awards in a place where your child can see them, such as on the refrigerator or a bedroom door. Children also enjoy stickers on the awards. Your child might want to do something special with the award, such as sending it to his/her grandmother, in order to receive additional recognition.

What are the two most important things to remember about the contract program?

The two most important things in this program are to never underestimate the power of positive reinforcement, and to provide recognition as soon as possible after the desired behavior has occurred. In situations where contract programs fail to produce positive behavior changes, it is often the result of giving a type of recognition that does not have meaning to the child, or delaying the recognition.

RECOGNITION SUGGESTIONS

KINDERGARTEN

RENT A VIDEO GAME
A RACE CAR
COLORED MARKERS
FAST FOOD LUNCH
PUPPET
RENT A MOVIE VIDEO
EXTRA TV TIME

CANDY
A NEW TOY
A BOOK
A TRUCK
MONEY
A BASEBALL HAT
A NEW GAME

DOLL ACCESSORIES
AN ACTION FIGURE
ICE CREAM
STICKERS
A COLORING BOOK
JEWELRY
EXTRA COMPUTER GAME TIME

FIRST GRADE

RENT A VIDEO GAME
GO OUT FOR DINNER
GO TO A BASEBALL GAME
CANDY
FAST FOOD LUNCH
A TOY CAR
CRAYONS
A MAGAZINE
A SPECIAL BOOK
A NEW DOLL

STICKERS
GO ON A BOAT
STAY UP LATER
JEWELRY
A KEY CHAIN
AN HOUR AT THE PARK
A FOOTBALL
ACTION FIGURES
DOLL ACCESSORIES
BASEBALL CARDS

CRAFT ITEMS
MONEY
HAVE A FRIEND SLEEP OVER
A COLORING BOOK
ACTION FIGURE ACCESSORIES
EXTRA TV TIME
A NEW GAME
PLAY MAKEUP
GOLDFISH

SECOND GRADE

RENT A VIDEO GAME
SPORTS CARDS
DAY OFF FROM SCHOOL
ACTION FIGURES
AN AWARD
TOY TRUCK
NEW GAME
PUZZLE
FAST FOOD LUNCH
STAY UP LATER
NEW BOOK
NEW VIDEO GAME
PIZZA DINNER
GO TO THE MOVIES

TOY CAR
COMPUTER GAME TIME
PEN
VIDEO TAPES
HAVE A FRIEND OVER
BASEBALL
RENT A MOVIE
DOLL
MONEY
CANDY
NEW TOY
DOLL ACCESSORIES
CANDY/GUM

EXTRA TV TIME
SLEEP-OVER WITH FRIENDS
EXTRA OUTDOORS TIME
BIRTHDAY PARTY
ICE CREAM
TRIP TO THE LIBRARY
BASEBALL HAT
NEW CLOTHES
WATERCOLOR PAINTS
STICKERS
KITTEN
NEW CRAYONS
STUFFED ANIMAL

THIRD GRADE

GO TO A MOVIE
CASSETTE TAPES
A NEW GAME
RENT A MOVIE
ACTION FIGURES
NEW BOOK
JEWELRY
ART SUPPLIES
ICE CREAM
VISIT MY COUSIN
PIZZA
RENT A VIDEO GAME
TOY BOAT
NEW WALLET
MORE ALLOWANCE
SPORTS ACCESSORIES
SEWING KIT

GO ROLLER-SKATING
DOLL ACCESSORIES
MONEY
BALL
COLORING BOOK
MARKERS
A POSTER
A HAMSTER
TRIP TO THE MALL
TRIP TO THE LIBRARY
CLOTHES
KITTEN OR PUPPY
TRIP TO THE ZOO
COMIC BOOKS
MAGAZINE
CRAYONS
TRIP TO A RESTAURANT

GUM/CANDY
LATER BEDTIME
NEW TOY
TOY CAR
FAST FOOD
HAVE FRIENDS SLEEP OVER
SPORTS CARDS
STAY OVERNIGHT WITH FRIEND
GO TO AN ARCADE
STICKER BOOK
STICKERS
GO TO A BASEBALL GAME
MORE VIDEO GAME TIME
GOLDFISH
PENS/PENCILS
GO TO A SWIMMING POOL
CRAFTS

FOURTH GRADE

FRIEND SLEEP OVER
JEWELRY/CRAFTS
MONEY
LATER BEDTIME
MARKERS
GO TO A FRIEND'S HOME
A YO-YO
TRIP TO THE MALL
GO FISHING
FILM FOR MY CAMERA
POSTERS
MUSIC CASSETTES
SPORTS CARD
MORE TV TIME
BOARD GAME

ICE CREAM
RENT VIDEO GAMES
JEWELRY
STICKERS
ACTION FIGURES
BLANK CASSETTE TAPES
PENS/PENCILS
GO TO THE ARCADE
NEW DOLL
SLEEP-OVER PARTY
PIZZA
BREAKFAST IN BED
NEW BOOK
NEW SHOES
TENNIS BALLS

MORE ALLOWANCE
FREEDOM FROM A CHORE
EXTRA PLAY TIME
CLOTHES
SPORTS EQUIPMENT
VISIT MY GRANDMOTHER
MORE VIDEO GAME TIME
GLOVES/MITTENS
PLAY A GAME WITH MY FAMILY
TICKETS TO A FOOTBALL GAME
KEYS TO THE HOUSE
RENT A VIDEO
CANDY/GUM
COMIC BOOKS
MORE OUTSIDE PLAY TIME

FOURTH GRADE

SLEEP LATE
NOTEBOOK
CASSETTES
PENCIL BOX
KARATE LESSONS

CRAYONS
COLORED PENCILS
WATCH
BIRTHDAY PARTY
GO OUT TO EAT

GOLDFISH
RADIO
GO TO A BASEBALL GAME
MAKEUP
CAR MODEL

FIFTH GRADE

STAY UP LATER
MOVIES
DAY OFF FROM SCHOOL
DAY OF NO HOMEWORK
ICE CREAM SUNDAE
NO CHORES FOR A WEEK
CABLE IN MY ROOM
SMALL RADIO
BASEBALL HAT
MAGAZINE
CLOTHES
ACTION FIGURES
MAKEUP
LIPSTICK
HAMSTER
BASKETBALL
WATER GUN
TRIP TO ARCADE
ROLLER-SKATING

MONEY
CASSETTE SINGLES
BOOKS
FOOTBALL
SPORTS CARDS
BLANK TAPES
CAKE
MOVIES WITH FRIENDS
FRIEND OVER FOR NIGHT
PET BIRD
GAS FOR DIRT BIKE
RENT A VIDEO GAME
NAIL POLISH
ART KIT
SLEEP LATE
RENT A VIDEO MOVIE
MORE PLAY TIME
POSTERS
GUM/CANDY

SWIMMING WITH FRIENDS
PIZZA PARTY
GAME
SLEEP OVER WITH FRIENDS
ONE HOUR OF TV IN BED
VISIT MY AUNT
ONE NIGHT UNTIL 1:00 AM
HIGHER ALLOWANCE
COMPUTER GAME
COMIC BOOKS
PERSONALIZED PENCILS
MILKSHAKE
JEWELRY/EARRINGS
HAIR BANDS
SPORTS MAGAZINE
CASSETTE TAPES
SPORTS EQUIPMENT
PARTY
HAIR ACCESSORIES

SIXTH GRADE

RENT A VIDEO GAME
HAVE A FRIEND SLEEP OVER
ALLOWANCE INCREASE
PIERCED EARS
A FRIEND OVER TO VISIT
JEWELRY
NEW MIRROR
MORE PHONE TIME
EARPHONES
MUSIC TAPE
DO HOMEWORK LATER
KITTEN
NEW NOTEBOOK
NEW MARKERS
HAT
HAIRSPRAY

STAY UP LATER
PLAY AFTER SCHOOL
A NEW HAIR CUT
COLORED PEN
ANY SMALL GIFT
SPORTS CARDS
PENS AND PENCILS
STUFFED ANIMAL
COMPUTER GAME
SEWING KIT
NEW BOOK
TRIP TO THE MALL
NEAT ERASERS
TAPE RACK
SCHOOL SUPPLIES
SHIRT

MORE PLAY TIME
HAIR ACCESSORIES
ICE CREAM
OUTING WITH FRIENDS
GO TO A FRIEND'S HOME
FLOWERS
EQUAL TREATMENT
NEW SNEAKERS
VIDEO GAME
ASSIGNMENT PAD
FAKE NAILS
CABLE TV
YO-YO
STICKERS
CLOTHES
PUZZLE

SEVENTH GRADE

STAY OUT LATER
MORE TIME WITH FRIENDS
BOWLING
MORE TIME OUTSIDE
SLEEP AT A FRIEND'S HOUSE
EXTRA TV TIME
REDO ROOM
GO OUT FOR DINNER
RENT A VIDEO GAME
RENT A COMPUTER GAME
PENS/PENCILS
NEW VIDEO GAME
SWEATPANTS/SWEATSHIRT
JEWELRY

ROLLER-SKATING
GO TO A MOVIE
MONEY
FOOTBALL
MORE PHONE TIME
TRIP TO THE ARCADE
MORE SCHOOL SUPPLIES
T-SHIRTS
PIZZA
POSTERS
HAIR ACCESSORIES
RENT A VIDEO MOVIE
MAGAZINES
CAT

DISCUSSIONS WITH PARENTS
GO TO THE MALL
STAY UP LATER
CASSETTE TAPES/CD'S
MORE ALLOWANCE
CLOTHES
SPORTS EQUIPMENT
COMIC BOOKS
GUM/CANDY
FRIENDS OVER TO VISIT
NEW HAT
SMALL PARTY
BOOKS
MAKEUP

EIGHTH GRADE

MONEY
STAY OUT LATER AT NIGHT
MORE ALLOWANCE
TRIP TO THE ARCADE
GO TO THE MOVIES
SATURDAY AT THE MALL
T-SHIRTS
SPORTS CARDS
NO CHORES FOR A WEEK
BOWLING
CD
RENT A VIDEO MOVIE
CLOTHES
PIZZA

JEWELRY
MORE PHONE TIME
SPORTS EQUIPMENT
EXCUSED FROM A CHORE
ROLLER-SKATING
A PARTY
CABLE IN MY ROOM
MAGAZINES
FAMILY DISCUSSIONS
MORE TIME WITH MOM
SAVINGS BOND
BOOK
CANDY
GO FISHING

GO OUT FOR DINNER
HAVE A FRIEND OVER
EXTRA PLAY TIME
FRIEND OVER TO SPEND NIGHT
CASSETTE TAPES
POSTERS
TIME OFF FROM BABY-SITTING
MORE ENCOURAGEMENT
NEW NOTEBOOK
HAIR ACCESSORIES
RIDE TO THE MALL
PERFUME
MAKEUP
STOCKS

GREAT WORK!

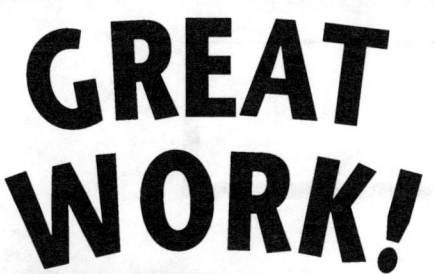

Earned by

_____

for

_____

_____

_____
SIGNED

_____
DATE

CERTIFICATE for COOPERATION

Earned by

_____

for

_____

_____

_____   _____
SIGNED   DATE

I'm Really Proud of You!

_____
SIGNED

_____
DATE

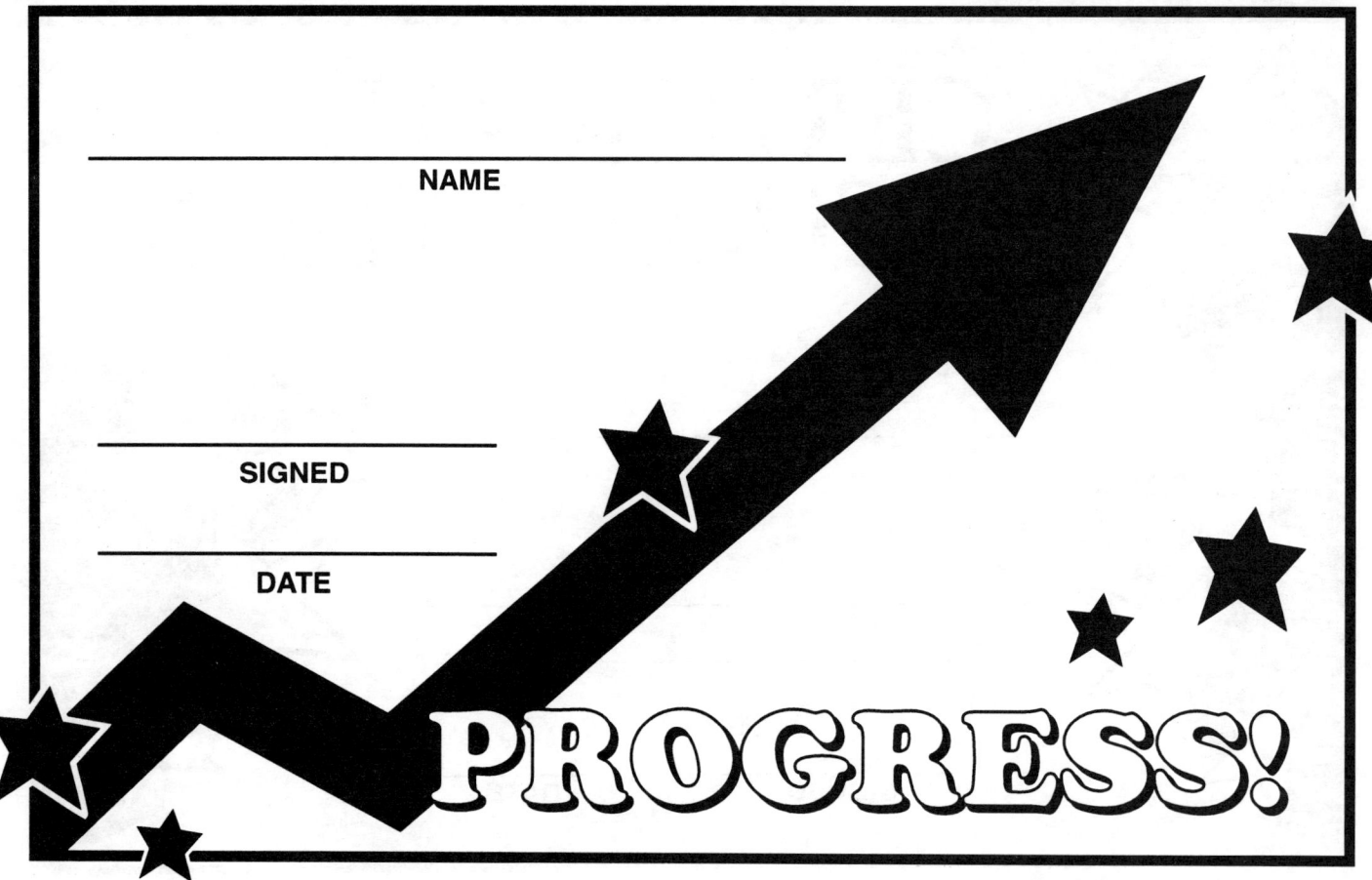

_____
NAME

_____
SIGNED

_____
DATE

PROGRESS!

SUPER STUDENT

_____
NAME

_____
SIGNED

_____
DATE

I KNEW THAT YOU COULD DO IT!

_____
SIGNED

_____
DATE

_____
NAME

Great Behavior!

Presented to:

_____

_____ _____
SIGNED   **DATE**

IMPROVEMENT AWARD

Presented to

_____

For

_____

_____

_____ _____
SIGNED   **DATE**